GROWN-UPS

A Child's Guide

Judith Marquiss

Copyright © 2023 Judith Marquiss
The moral right of the author has been asserted.

Apart from any fair dealing for the purposes of research or private study, or criticism or review, as permitted under the Copyright, Designs and Patents Act 1988, this publication may only be reproduced, stored or transmitted, in any form or by any means, with the prior permission in writing of the publishers, or in the case of reprographic reproduction in accordance with the terms of licences issued by the Copyright Licensing Agency. Enquiries concerning reproduction outside those terms should be sent to the publishers.

Matador
Unit E2 Airfield Business Park,
Harrison Road, Market Harborough,
Leicestershire. LE16 7UL
Tel: 0116 279 2299
Email: books@troubador.co.uk
Web: www.troubador.co.uk/matador
Twitter: @matadorbooks

ISBN 978-1-80514-034-4

British Library Cataloguing in Publication Data.
A catalogue record for this book is available from the British Library.

Typeset in 24pt Chalkduster by Troubador Publishing Ltd, Leicester, UK

Matador is an imprint of Troubador Publishing Ltd

For
Jodie, Olivia, Marley, Thea,
Freya and Soren,

with love

Grown-ups sometimes need a lot of workers to help them with all their jobs.

Making furniture for the home can be hard work.

Oh dear!
What a mess in the kitchen.

Look what has happened to the garden after a holiday!

You can colour this page in if you would like to.

Grown-ups need to keep fit.

Look at all the different busy jobs that grown-ups do as well as looking after you.

Sometimes grown-ups need time to relax.

Grown-ups try to make a home for you, whether it is in a castle, a caravan, a tent or a cottage.

You can colour this page in if you would like to.

No matter how busy your grown-ups are, they still love to play with you.

BV - #0029 - 140623 - C22 - 210/297/2 - PB - 9781805140344 - Gloss Lamination